AF539273

To Rachel: July, 1985

Warm all the kitchen with Thy love,
and light it with Thy peace
Forgive me all my worrying
and make my grumbling cease.
Thou who didst love to give men food,
in room or by the sea
Accept this service that I do,
I do it unto thee.

This is a little prayer I have hanging in my kitchen. I wanted to share it with you— because I love you—

Grandma Sampson.

RULES FOR GOOD COOKS

Wash your hands.

Put on your apron.

Read your recipe carefully.

Place everything you need on the kitchen table.

Have mother teach you how to use the stove.

Measure everything very carefully.

Wash your dishes.

Sweep the kitchen and leave it in order.

Level all measurements like this.

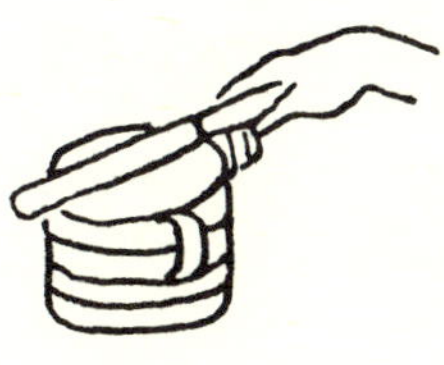

ISBN 0-931018-01-3

Printed in the United States of America

Published by:
Cogan Books
4332 Artesia
Fullerton, CA 92633

Library of Congress Cataloging in Publication Data

Evans, Eleanor, 1932-
For good measure.

SUMMARY: Simple recipes for breakfast, sandwiches, main dishes, breads, salads, cookies, desserts, candy, drinks, and "this 'n that."

1. Cookery--Juvenile literature. [1. Cookery]
I. Butcher, Lindsay. II. Title.
TX652.5.E82 641.5 78-13590
ISBN 0-931018-01-3

Originally published by Two Step Books.

FOR GOOD MEASURE
a cookbook for children

by
Eleanor Evans

Illustrated by
Lindsey Butcher

Cogan Books, Fullerton, California

CONTENTS

Hotcakes

½ cup flour of

¼ teaspoon salt of

1½ teaspoons baking powder of

1 tablespoon sugar of

1 egg, beaten

½ cup milk of

1 tablespoon shortening of

Put frying pan on burner. Heat until a few drops of water sizzle when added. Make sure the pan is oiled or buttered.

Sift dry ingredients together including sugar.

In a small bowl, mix egg, milk and shortening.

Add liquids to dry ingredients and mix well.

Drop batter from spoon into heated pan. Cook until bubbles form, flip to other side and brown. You can make these any size you want.

Serve with butter and syrup.

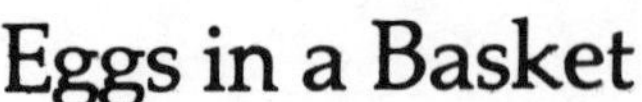

Eggs in a Basket

1 slice bread

1 tablespoon butter or bacon grease   of BUTTER

1 egg

Cut a small hole in center of bread about the size of an egg yolk.
Heat butter in a small skillet. When foamy, add slice of bread.
Break egg into hole.
Cover and cook slowly until egg white is set.
Turn over and cook lightly for a few seconds.

Scrambled Up Eggs

2 eggs

1 teaspoon water

1 tablespoon butter

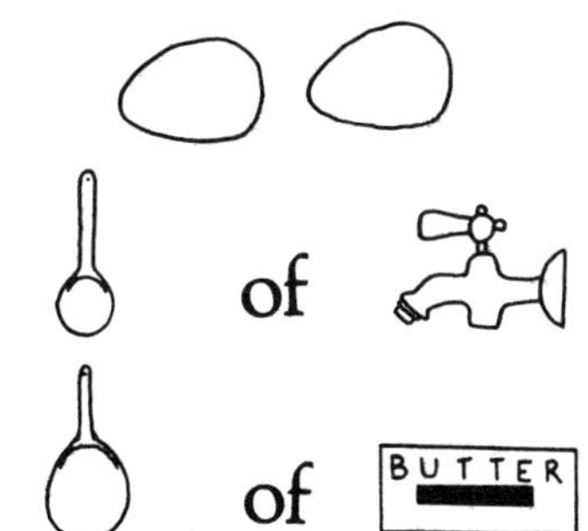

Beat eggs and water until blended but not foamy.
Heat butter in skillet until it foams.
Add eggs and stir quickly until firm.

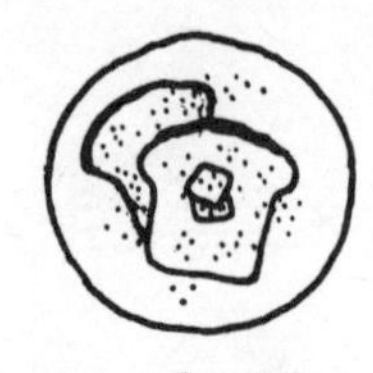

French Toast

1 egg

1 tablespoon milk

dash of vanilla

2 tablespoons butter

2 slices stale French bread

Whip egg, milk and vanilla together until well blended.
Dip both sides of bread into egg mixture.
Heat butter in skillet until foamy. Fry the bread 2 to 3 minutes on each side until golden brown.
Sprinkle with powdered sugar and serve with butter and syrup.

Popovers

1 egg	
½ cup milk	of MILK
½ cup flour	of XXX
pinch of salt	pinch of SALT

Crack egg into bowl.
Add milk and beat with eggbeater until blended.
Add flour and salt and stir with wooden spoon.
Try to get some of the lumps out, but don't worry if there are a few left.
Pour batter into greased muffin tins, half full and place in cold oven.
Turn to 450 and bake for 30 minutes. Don't peek.
Makes 4.

Cinnamon Toast

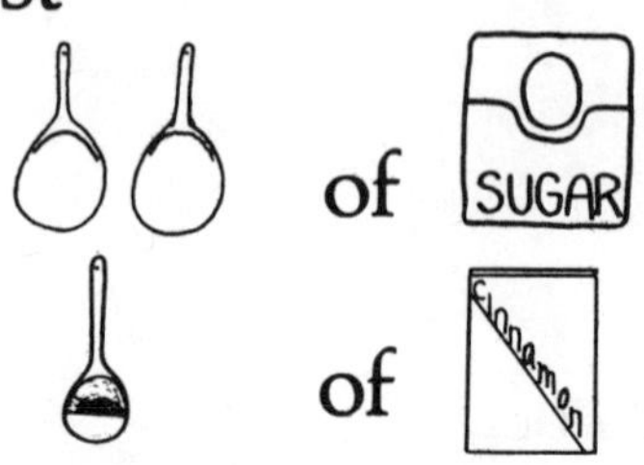

2 tablespoons sugar

½ teaspoon cinnamon

Mix sugar and cinnamon together. Shake over buttered toast.

Honey Butter

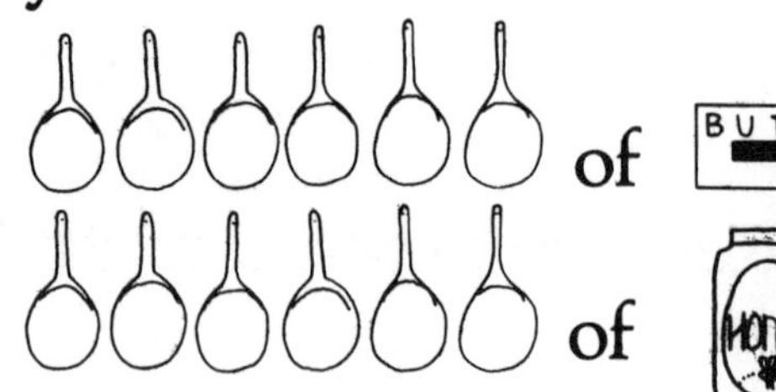

6 tablespoons soft butter

6 tablespoons honey

Cream butter until fluffy.
Cream in honey until light.
Store in refrigerator.

Cheese Muffins

½ cup shredded Cheddar cheese

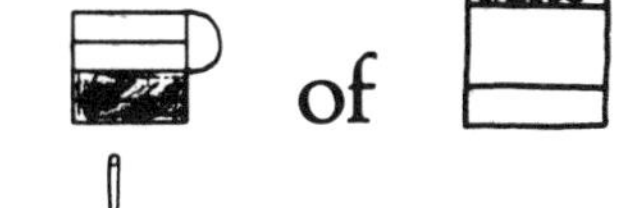

1 tablespoon sliced olives

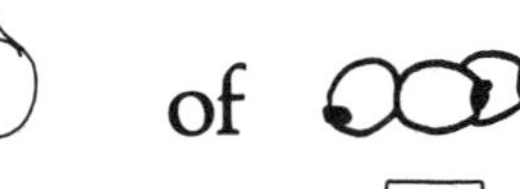

1 tablespoon mayonnaise

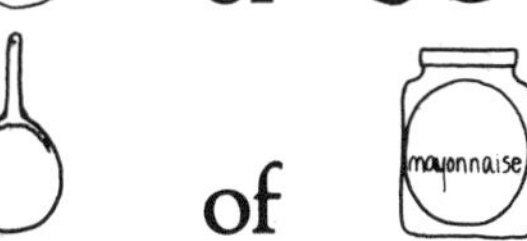

1 English muffin

In a small bowl, mix cheese, olives and mayonnaise. Put on top of half a buttered English muffin. Put under broiler until cheese has melted.

Eat right away.

Fisherman's Tuna Sandwich

1 can tuna

1 tablespoon sweet pickle relish 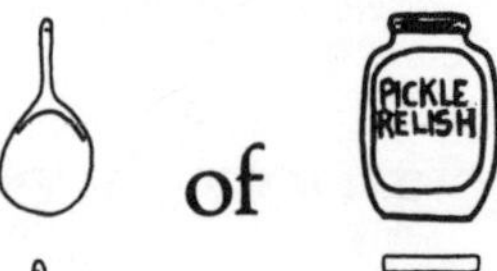

3 to 4 tablespoons mayonnaise 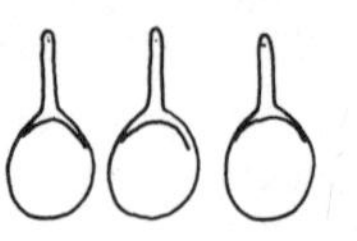 of 

Drain tuna.
Put in a small bowl and break up with a fork.
Add pickle relish and mayonnaise, mix well.
Keep in refrigerator.

Fried Egg Sandwich

1 egg

1 teaspoon finely sliced onion of

1 teaspoon finely chopped green pepper of

1 tablespoon butter or bacon grease of BUTTER

Heat bacon grease or butter in a small skillet.
Break egg into skillet. Break the yolk.
Sprinkle onion and green pepper on top.
Cook egg 2 to 3 minutes, turn over and brown the other side.
Put on buttered bread. Try lettuce and mayonnaise with this sandwich.

Grilled Cheese Sandwich

1 slice American or Cheddar cheese

2 slices bread

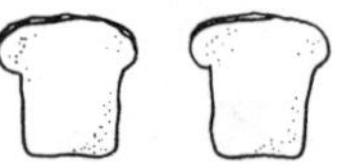

butter

Butter one side of each bread slice.
Put cheese between unbuttered sides.
Heat a skillet on medium heat. When hot, cook sandwich until toasty brown on both sides. Remove when cheese has melted.

Honey Peanut Butter Spread

4 tablespoons honey 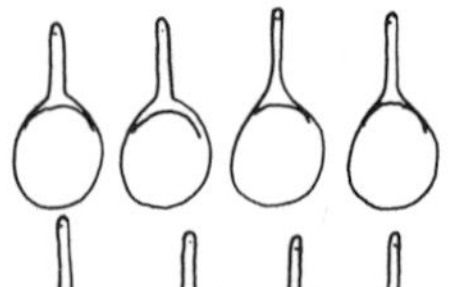 of 

4 tablespoons peanut butter of 

Mix ingredients in a bowl until blended.
Makes enough for 2 sandwiches.

Tuna Noodle Bake

6 ounces noodles

2 teaspoons salt

1 seven ounce can tuna, drained

1 can cream of mushroom soup

1 cup milk

1 cup crushed potato chips

Preheat oven to 350.
Cook noodles in 2 quarts boiling water with salt for 10 minutes.
Drain, rinse with hot water, drain.
Pour into buttered 9 by 9 baking dish.
Spread tuna on top.
Mix soup and milk together, pour over top.
Top with potato chips.
Bake at 350 for 25 to 30 minutes.

Old Fashioned Meatloaf

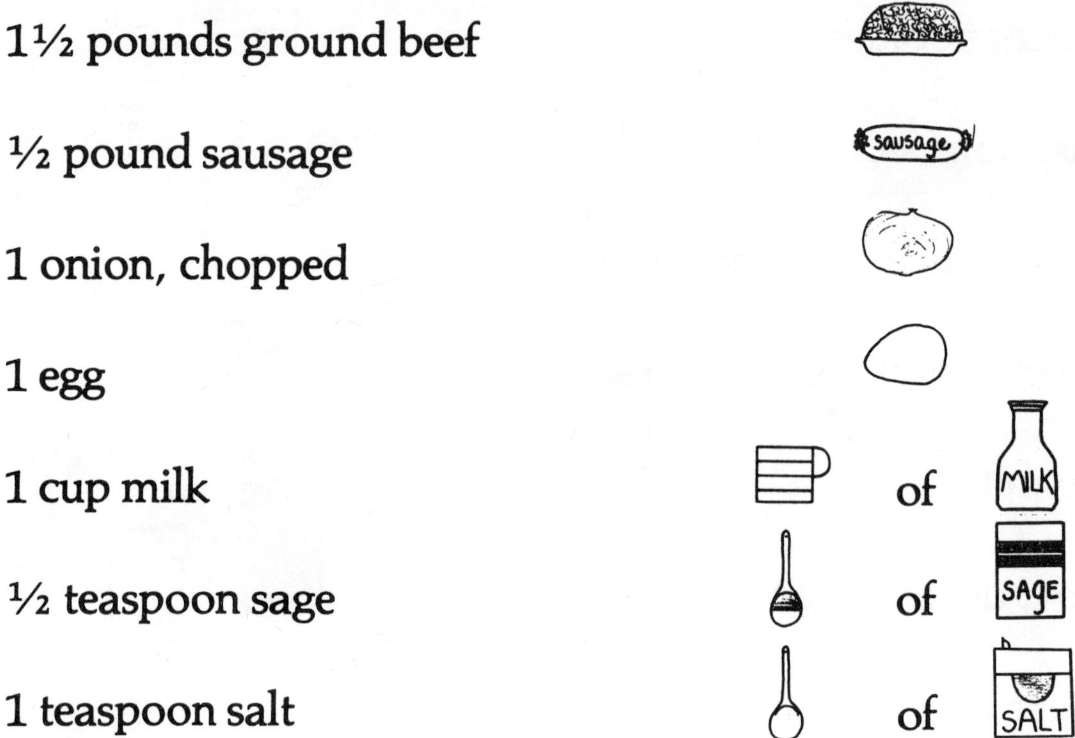

1½ pounds ground beef

½ pound sausage

1 onion, chopped

1 egg

1 cup milk

½ teaspoon sage

1 teaspoon salt

Preheat oven to 350.
Beat egg with milk, add sage and salt.
Put everything into a large bowl and mix with a fork until well blended.
Put into 9 by 5 loaf pan.
Bake at 350 for 1½ hours.
Cold meatloaf is good in sandwiches.

Sloppy Joe

½ pound ground beef 

½ onion, chopped 

1 tablespoon shortening  of 

⅓ cup catsup  of 

1 teaspoon prepared mustard  of 

1½ teaspoons vinegar  of 

1 teaspoon sugar  of 

1½ teaspoons Worcestershire sauce 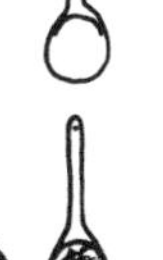 of

2 hamburger buns  

Brown meat and onion in shortening in a skillet.
Add remaining ingredients (except buns).
Cover and simmer for 10 to 15 minutes, stirring from time to time.
Spoon onto hamburger buns. You may toast them if you want.

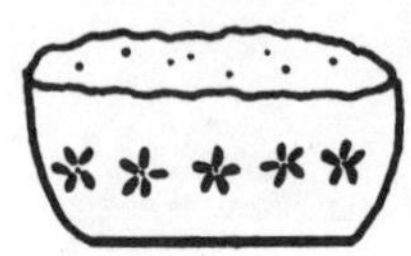

Chili 'n Cornbread

1 pound ground beef

1/3 cup chopped onion of

2 teaspoons chili powder of

1/4 teaspoon salt of

1 teaspoon Worcestershire sauce of

1 1/2 cups canned tomatoes of

1 cup drained kidney beans of

1 recipe corn muffins

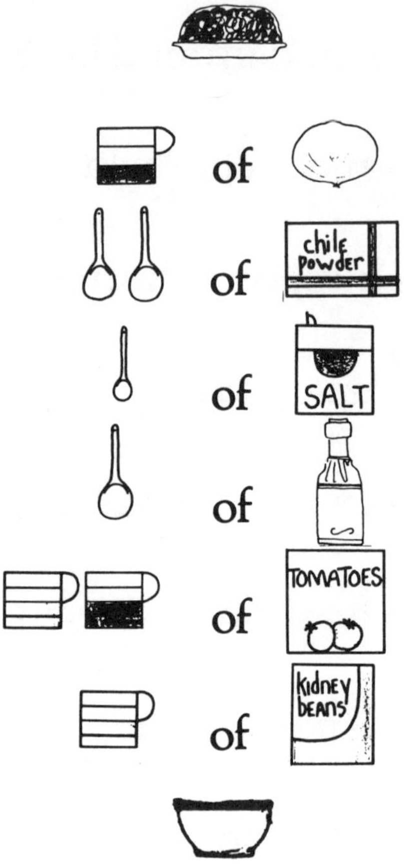

Preheat oven to 400.
Brown meat and onions in skillet.
Add seasoning and tomatoes. Cover and simmer for 10 minutes. Stir several times.
Add beans, mix well. Pour into buttered casserole. Top with corn muffin batter, spreading it evenly on the top.
Bake at 400 for 20 minutes.

Featherlight Corn Muffins

4 tablespoons butter		of
½ cup flour		of
4 tablespoons yellow cornmeal		of
2 tablespoons sugar		of
1 teaspoon baking powder		of
pinch of salt	pinch	of
1 egg		
2 tablespoons milk		of

Preheat oven to 350.
Melt butter over low heat. Set aside to cool.
Sift dry ingredients together into a bowl.
Beat egg and milk together in another bowl.
Stir butter and egg mixture into flour.
Fill paper baking cups in muffin pan half full of batter.
Bake at 350 for 15 minutes.

Baking powder Biscuits

1 cup flour

¼ teaspoon salt

2 teaspoons baking powder

2 tablespoons shortening

⅓ cup milk

Preheat oven to 450.
Sift dry ingredients together.
Cut in shortening with a fork until crumbly.
Add milk and stir just until the dough stays together.
Put on a lightly floured board or wax paper and pat until ½ inch thick.
Cut with round biscuit cutter and place on ungreased cookie sheet.
Bake at 450 for 12 to 15 minutes.
Makes 4 biscuits.

Bran Muffins

1 cup stone ground whole wheat flour — of

½ cup bran cereal — of

2 teaspoons baking powder — of

1 teaspoon soda — of

½ teaspoon salt — of

½ cup sugar — of

6 tablespoons vegetable oil — of

1 cup milk — of

1 egg, well beaten

⅓ cup raisins — of

Mix all dry ingredients including sugar in a large bowl.
Stir in oil, milk and beaten egg.
Mix well. Add raisins.
Put in covered container in refrigerator overnight.
Fill paper baking cups in a muffin pan half full.
Bake at 375 for 15 minutes.
Batter will keep in refrigerator for 2 weeks.

Hopscotch Scones

1 cup flour

3 tablespoons soft butter

½ teaspoon salt

2 tablespoons sugar

3 teaspoons baking powder

1 egg

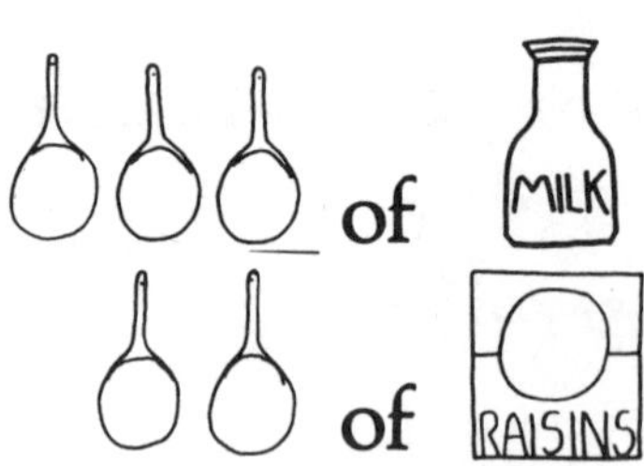

3 tablespoons milk

2 tablespoons currants or raisins

Preheat oven to 350.
Cut butter into flour with pastry blender or fork until crumbly.
Add salt, sugar and baking powder.
Beat egg in a small bowl. Add milk.
Add egg mixture to flour and mix gently. Add currants.
Drop dough from spoon onto buttered cookie sheet.
Bake at 350 for 12 to 15 minutes.
Serve with butter and jam.
Makes 4.

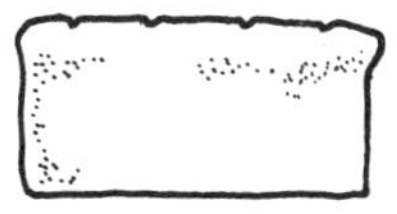

Rainyday White Bread

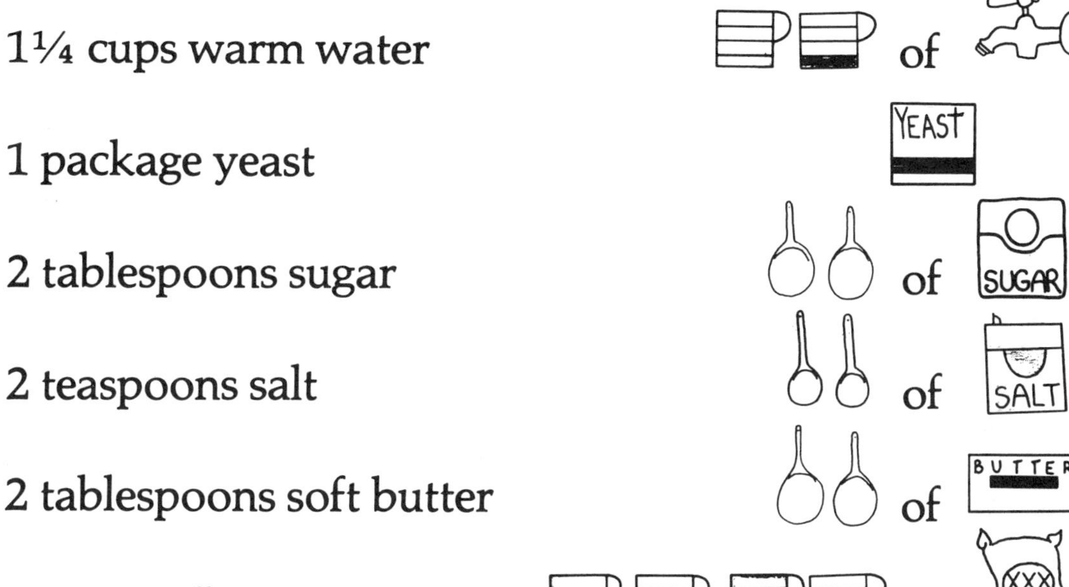

1¼ cups warm water

1 package yeast

2 tablespoons sugar

2 teaspoons salt

2 tablespoons soft butter

3¼ cups flour

Put warm water in a warmed mixing bowl. Sprinkle yeast over it and stir until dissolved.
Add sugar, salt, butter and 1½ cups flour.
Beat 2 minutes at medium speed, mixing well.
Stir in remaining 1¾ cups flour and mix until smooth.
Cover with a cloth and let sit in a warm place to rise until double in bulk: 30 to 40 minutes.
Punch dough down, knead lightly for 2 minutes.
Shape into a loaf and put in buttered 9 by 5 loaf pan.
Cover and let rise until doubled: 40 to 60 minutes. Poke a finger into dough. If hole remains the dough has doubled.
Bake at 375 for 45 to 55 minutes.
Take out of pan and cool before slicing.

Anytime Applesauce

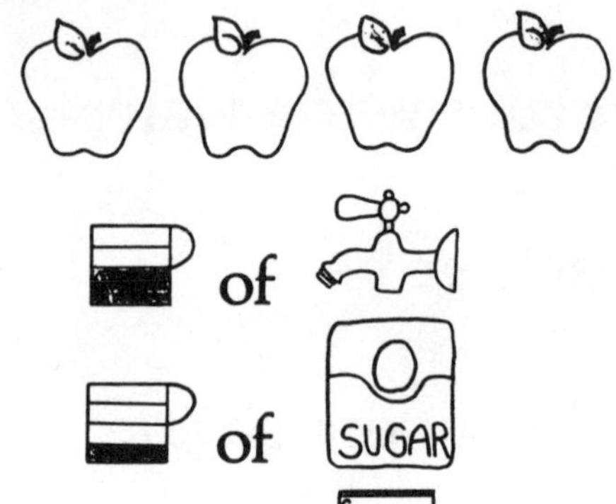

4 green apples

½ cup water

¼ cup sugar

pinch of cinnamon

pinch of 

Peel apples, cut into quarters and core.
Put apples in saucepan, add water.
Cover and cook slowly for 15 to 20 minutes until apples are soft.
Remove from heat, mash with a fork.
Add sugar and cinnamon, put back on heat and simmer for 2 minutes.
Serve hot or cold.

Rainbow Fruit Salad

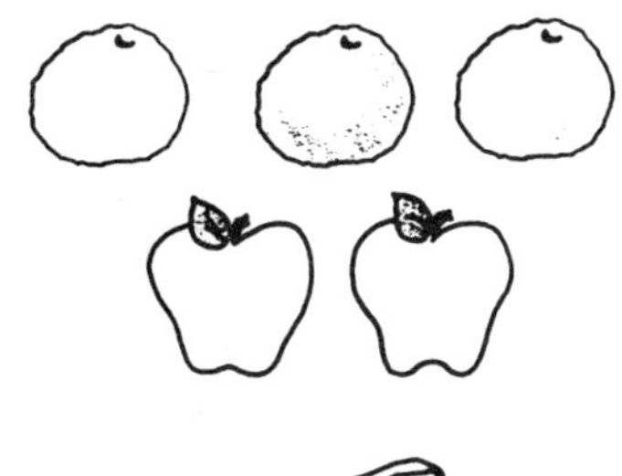

3 oranges

2 apples

1 banana

Peel and slice two oranges.
Core and chop apples.
Peel and slice banana.
Mix all fruit into a bowl.
Quarter the third orange and squeeze juice over mixed fruit.
You can add other kinds of fruit.
1 cup sliced strawberries
1 cup melon cubes
1 cup grapes
Choose one of your favorites.

Creamy French Dressing

½ teaspoon salt

½ teaspoon sugar

½ teaspoon dry mustard

½ cup vegetable oil

2 tablespoons apple cider vinegar

3 tablespoons catsup

Place all ingredients in blender.
Blend until creamy.
Serve over lettuce.

Brownies

4 squares unsweetened chocolate

½ cup butter

2 eggs

1 cup sugar

¾ cup flour

¼ teaspoon salt

1 teaspoon vanilla

¼ cup chopped walnuts

of BUTTER
of SUGAR
of XXX
of SALT
of VANILLA
of walnuts

Preheat oven to 350.
Melt chocolate and butter over low heat.
Beat eggs until light in a medium bowl.
Beat in sugar.
Sift in dry ingredients. Mix well. Add vanilla and chocolate/butter mixture. Stir in walnuts.
Bake in buttered 9 by 9 baking pan at 350 for 20 to 25 minutes.
Cool and cut into squares.

Gingersnaps

6 tablespoons shortening		of
½ cup sugar		of
2 tablespoons molasses		of
1 egg		
1 cup flour		of
pinch of salt	pinch	of
1 teaspoon soda		of
½ teaspoon cinnamon		of
½ teaspoon cloves		of
1 teaspoon ginger		of

Preheat oven to 350.
Cream shortening and sugar until light and fluffy.
Add molasses and egg. Mix well.
Sift in dry ingredients together. Mix well.
Roll into walnut sized balls, roll balls in sugar.
Bake on ungreased cookie sheet at 350 for 10 to 12 minutes.

Oatmeal Crunchies

6 tablespoons shortening of

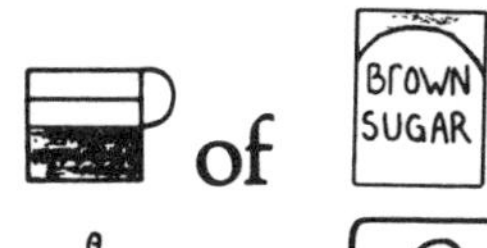

½ cup packed brown sugar of

4 tablespoons sugar of

1 egg

½ teaspoon vanilla of

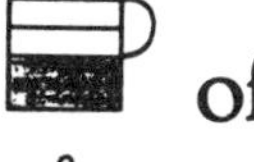

½ cup flour of

½ teaspoon salt of

¼ teaspoon soda of

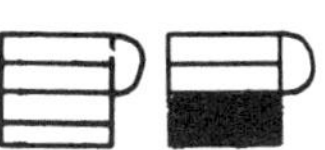

1½ cups oatmeal of

Preheat oven to 350.
Cream shortening and sugars together.
Beat in egg and vanilla until smooth.
Sift in flour, salt and soda.
Mix well. Stir in oatmeal.
Drop by spoonfuls onto ungreased cookie sheet. Bake at 350 for 12 to 15 minutes.
You can add raisins or chocolate chips to these.

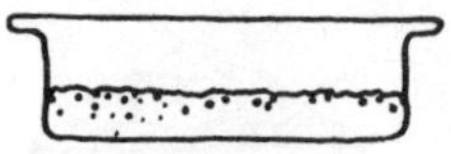

Kookie Brittle

½ cup sugar

½ teaspoon salt

½ cup soft butter or margarine

1 teaspoon vanilla

1 cup flour

½ cup semisweet chocolate chips

Preheat oven to 375.
Mix sugar and salt together. Cream in butter. Add vanilla. Sift in flour. Mix until crumbly. Stir in chocolate chips. Pat into ungreased 9 by 9 baking pan. Bake at 375 for 25 minutes.
Cool in pan. Break into irregular pieces.

Rice Krispie Cookies

4 tablespoons butter or margarine  of 

10¼ ounces little marshmallows (1 bag) 

5 cups Rice Krispies  of 

Melt butter in a big pot.
Add marshmallows and stir with a wooden spoon until melted.
Add cereal and stir until well mixed.
Pat into buttered 9 by 12 pan.
Refrigerate until firm.

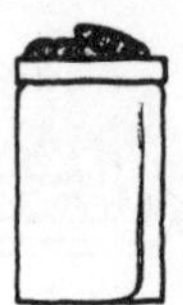

Mr. Peanut's Butter Cookies

½ cup butter or margarine

1 cup brown sugar

½ cup crunchy peanut butter

1 egg

2 tablespoons milk

1 teaspoon vanilla

1¾ cups flour

1 teaspoon baking soda

½ teaspoon salt

Preheat oven to 350.
Cream butter and sugar until light.
Mix in peanut butter.
Beat in egg, milk and vanilla.
Sift dry ingredients together into batter. Mix well.
Roll into walnut sized balls. Roll balls in sugar.
Press down with a fork onto ungreased cookie sheet.
Bake at 350 for 8 to 10 minutes.

Butterscotch Squares

1½ cups flour

½ teaspoon salt

2 teaspoons baking powder

2 cups brown sugar

½ cup butter or margarine

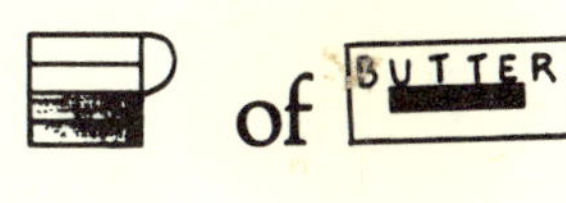

2 eggs

1½ teaspoons vanilla

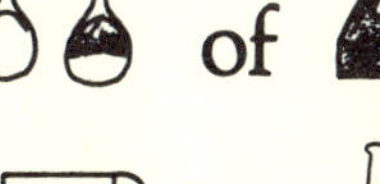

½ cup chopped walnuts

Preheat oven to 325.
Sift flour, salt and baking powder together.
Add sugar.
Melt butter and mix in.
Beat in eggs.
Stir in vanilla and nuts.
Bake in buttered 9 by 9 pan at 325 for 40 minutes.
Cool and cut into squares.

Sweet Lemon Treats

1 cup flour

¼ cup powdered sugar

½ cup soft butter

2 eggs

¾ cup sugar

3 tablespoons lemon juice

2 tablespoons flour

½ teaspoon baking powder

¼ cup powdered sugar

Preheat oven to 350.
Sift flour and sugar into medium bowl.
Cut in butter with a pastry blender or fork until crumbly.
Pat into 9 by 9 buttered pan. Bake at 350 for 12 to 15 minutes.

Beat eggs with beater until very light and lemon colored.

Beat in sugar and lemon juice.

Sift in flour and baking powder. Mix.

Pour over baked crust. Bake at 350 for 20 minutes.

Remove from oven and sift ¼ cup powdered sugar over the top. Cool and cut into squares.

Good and Fudgey Pie

2 eggs	
1 cup sugar	of SUGAR
½ cup soft butter or margarine	of BUTTER
½ cup flour	of XXX
4 tablespoons cocoa	of COCOA
1 teaspoon vanilla	of VANILLA
pinch of salt	pinch of SALT
½ cup chopped walnuts	of walnuts

Preheat oven to 325.
Put everything except the nuts in a medium bowl.
Beat for 4 minutes. Stir in nuts.
Pour into buttered pie pan.
Bake at 325 for 30 minutes.
Serve with whipped cream or ice cream.

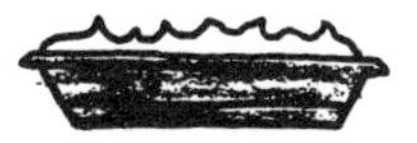

Walnutty Pie

20 saltine crackers

1 teaspoon baking powder of

½ cup chopped or ground walnuts of

3 egg whites whites of

1 scant cup sugar of

1 teaspoon vanilla of

Preheat oven to 325.
Put crackers in a plastic bag and crush with a rolling pin until fine.
Mix crackers, baking powder and nuts in a bowl.
In another bowl, beat egg whites until stiff, not dry.
Slowly add sugar and beat until glossy.
Fold nut and cracker mixture into egg whites. Stir in vanilla.
Pour into buttered pie pan.
Bake at 325 for 30 to 35 minutes. Serve with whipped cream.

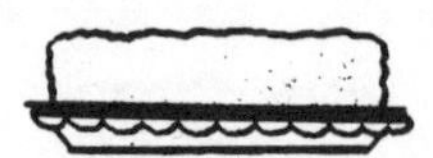

Wacky Cake

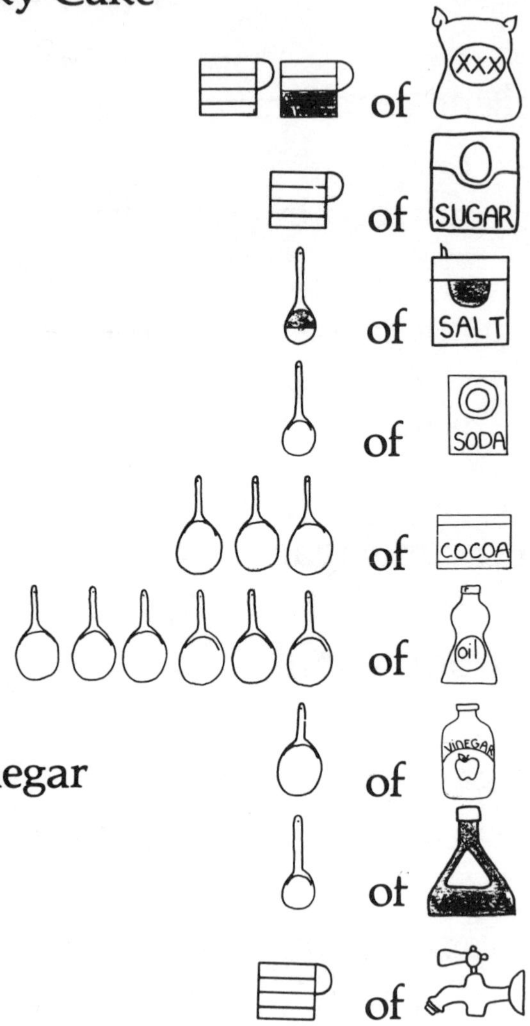

1½ cups flour

1 cup sugar

½ teaspoon salt

1 teaspoon soda

3 tablespoons cocoa

6 tablespoons vegetable oil

1 tablespoon apple cider vinegar

1 teaspoon vanilla

1 cup cold water

Preheat oven to 350.
Sift all dry ingredients into an ungreased 9 by 9 pan.
Make a well in the center and pour the oil, vinegar, vanilla and cold water into it.
Mix well with a fork until smooth.
Bake at 350 for 25 to 30 minutes.
Cool and frost with chocolate frosting.

Chocolate Frosting

3 tablespoons cocoa

1 cup powdered sugar

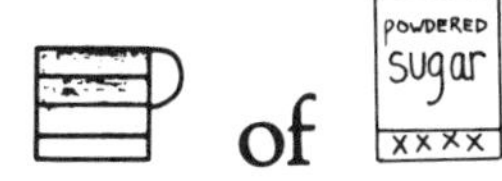

2 tablespoons soft butter

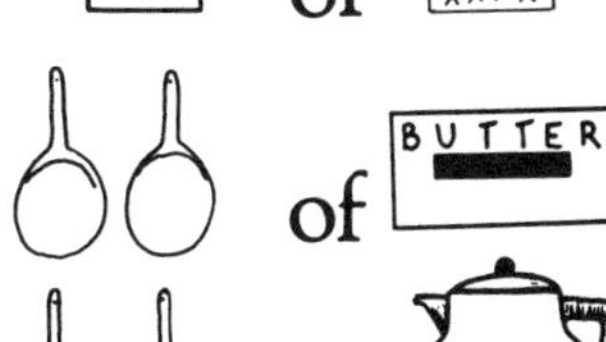

2 tablespoons hot coffee of

Sift cocoa and sugar together into a bowl.
Add butter.
Add hot coffee and beat until thick and smooth.

Spicy Applesauce Cupcakes

3 tablespoons butter 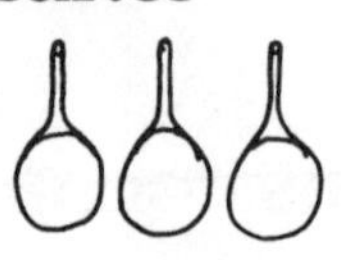 of 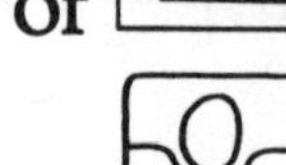

¼ cup sugar  of 

¼ cup brown sugar, firmly packed  of 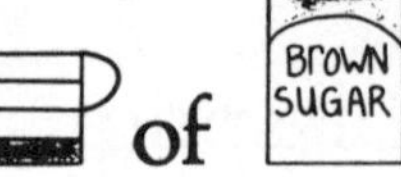

1 egg 

¼ teaspoon vanilla  of 

⅔ cup flour  of

½ teaspoon baking powder  of 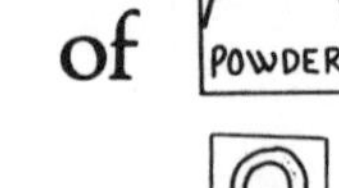

¼ teaspoon soda 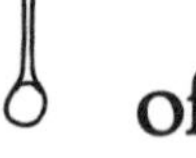 of

½ teaspoon cinnamon 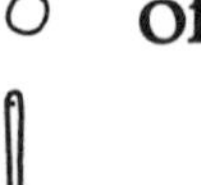 of 

¼ teaspoon cloves  of

pinch of salt — pinch of 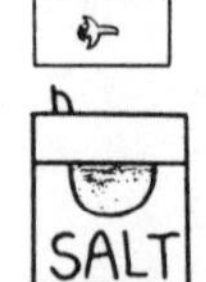

⅓ cup applesauce 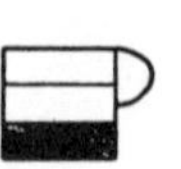 of 

Preheat oven to 350.
Cream butter and sugars together.
Beat in egg and vanilla.
Sift in dry ingredients, mixed together.
Mix in applesauce.
Fill paper baking cups in muffin pan half full.
Bake at 350 for 20 to 25 minutes.

Peach Crumble

1 can sliced peaches (1 pound, 13 ounces)

¼ cup peach syrup

6 tablespoons flour

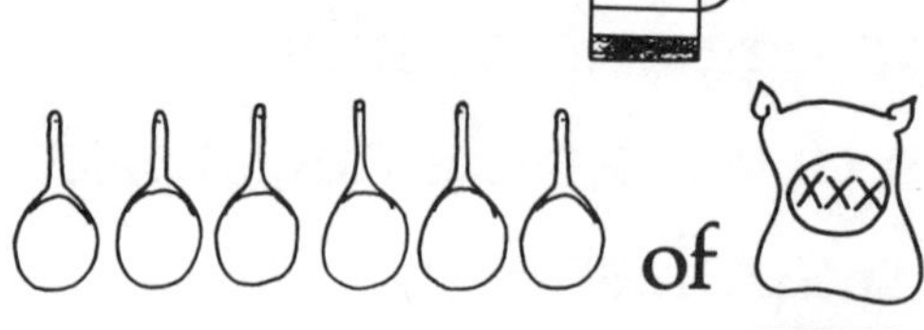

¼ cup brown sugar

of

pinch of nutmeg

pinch of

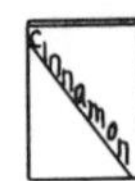

¼ teaspoon cinnamon

of

3 tablespoons butter

of

Preheat oven to 350.
Drain peaches, saving the syrup and put into a 9 by 9 baking pan.
Pour ¼ cup syrup over peaches.
Mix flour, sugar and spices together. Cut in butter with a fork until crumbly.
Sprinkle on top of peaches.
Bake at 350 for 25 to 30 minutes.

Chocolate Pudding

⅓ cup sugar	of SUGAR
2 teaspoons cornstarch	of cornstarch
pinch of salt	pinch of SALT
1 egg yolk	yolk of
1 cup milk	 of MILK
½ teaspoon vanilla	of VANILLA
1½ squares unsweetened chocolate	

Mix sugar, cornstarch, salt and egg yolk in a saucepan.

In another saucepan, heat the milk over medium heat just until it bubbles. Make sure it doesn't boil.

Stir milk into sugar mixture. Cook over medium heat, stirring constantly, until it thickens.

Remove from heat, add vanilla. Break chocolate into pieces and stir into custard until chocolate has melted.

You can eat this warm or cold.

Chocolate Munchies

1 six ounce package semisweet chocolate chips 

½ cup salted peanuts  of 

1 cup chow mein noodles  of 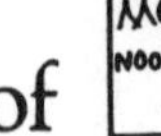

Melt chocolate over very low heat.
Stir in nuts and noodles. Toss gently to blend.
Drop by spoonfuls onto waxed paper.
Chill to harden.

Fudge

3 six ounce packages semisweet chocolate chips

1 can sweetened condensed milk

pinch of salt

1½ teaspoons vanilla

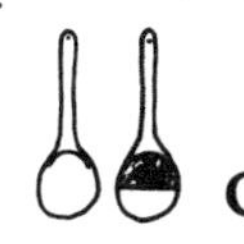

Melt chocolate over very low heat.
Remove from heat. Add sweetened condensed milk, salt and vanilla.
Stir only until smooth.
Spread onto buttered plate and refrigerate until firm; about 2 hours.
Cut into squares.

Lemonade

⅔ cup water — of

⅔ cup sugar

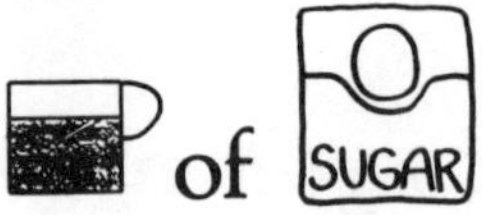

⅔ cup lemon juice (3 to 4 lemons)

2½ cups cold water

Put water and sugar in a saucepan and stir. Boil for 1 to 2 minutes and cool.
Squeeze lemons and pour juice into a pitcher.
Add 2½ cups cold water and cooled syrup and mix well.
Pour into glasses with lots of ice cubes.

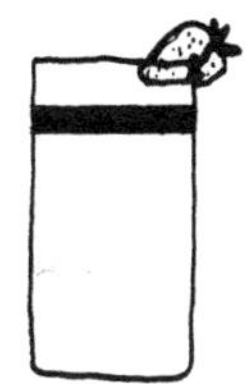

Strawberry Pineapple Crush

12 ounces pineapple juice (1 can)

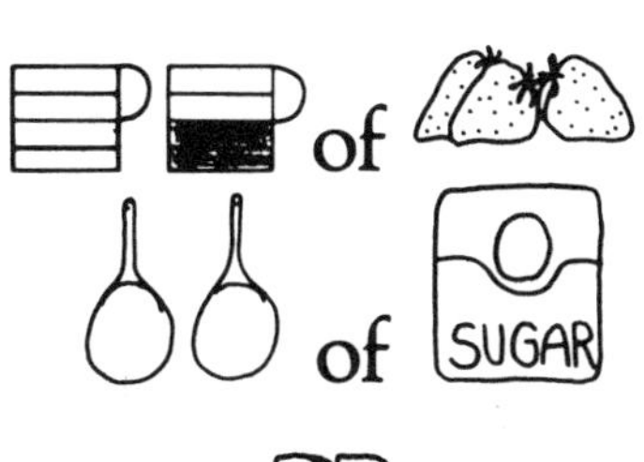

1½ cups strawberries

2 tablespoons sugar

6 to 8 ice cubes

Place all ingredients in a blender and blend.

Banana Smoothie

1 banana

1 cup milk

1 scoop vanilla ice cream

Place all ingredients in blender.
Blend until creamy.

Cocoa Mix

2 tablespoons cocoa

2 tablespoons sugar

½ cup dried milk

Mix all together. Store covered.

Put 3 to 4 tablespoons of mix in a cup, and add boiling water. Stir well.

Old Time Strawberry Jam

2 cups strawberries — of

2 cups sugar — of

Wash strawberries, hull and cut in half. Measure 2 full cups.

Put strawberries and sugar in a large saucepan, stir well and let sit for 5 minutes.

Place on heat, bring to a boil, stirring.

Turn down heat and simmer for 40 minutes, stirring often.

Cool slightly, skim the foam from the top. (It's good to eat.)

Pour jam into jar and let stand uncovered until cold, to thicken.

Cover and refrigerate.

Gelatin Blocks

1 package flavored gelatin

1 envelope unflavored gelatin

 of 

1¾ cups water

Mix gelatins together in a saucepan.
Stir in ¾ cup water, heat, stirring constantly until the gelatin is dissolved.
Add 1 cup cold water and stir.
Put in 9 by 5 pan, refrigerate until firm.
Cut into small squares.

Deviled Eggs

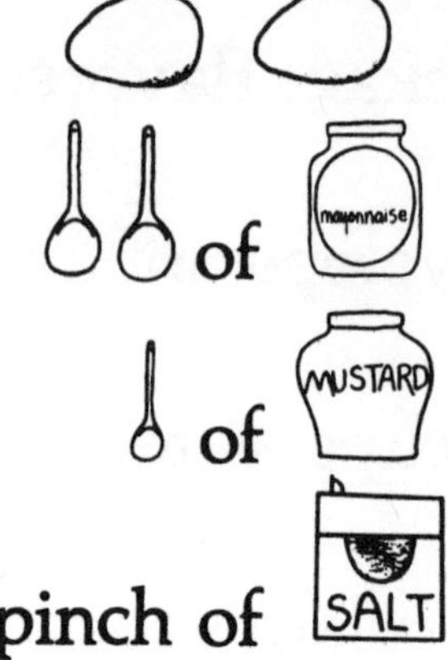

2 eggs

2 teaspoons mayonnaise

¼ teaspoon prepared mustard

pinch of salt

paprika

Put eggs in a small saucepan, cover with cold water, bring to a boil.

Turn heat down to barely simmering and cook eggs for 15 minutes.

Pour off hot water and run cold water over eggs until cold.

Shell eggs.

Carefully cut eggs in half.

Put yolks in a small bowl and mash well with a fork. Add mustard, mayonnaise and salt. Mix well.

Refill egg whites with yolks, using a spoon.

Sprinkle with paprika.

Modeling Dough #1

1 cup baking soda

½ cup cornstarch

½ cup plus 2 tablespoons cold water

Mix everything in a saucepan.
Bring to a boil, boil 1 minute until it looks like mashed potatoes.
Put on waxed paper and knead for a few minutes.
Keep in a plastic bag in the refrigerator.
If you want to paint it, let it dry for 1 or 2 days first.

Modeling Dough #2

1 cup flour

½ cup salt

½ cup water

Mix flour and salt in a bowl.
Slowly add water and mix until blended, but not sticky.
Knead for 10 minutes.
You can add food coloring to the water if you want a color.
Keep in a plastic bag in the refrigerator.
Can be baked at 325 for 30 minutes for each ¼ inch of thickness if you paint it.

My Own Recipes

Put Peanut Butter to cover the slic of bread. to slices of Bread.

then tost untill Brown then after you can put Jam on if youed like.

My Own Recipes

My Own Recipes

My Own Recipes

My Own Recipes

My Own Recipes

My Own Recipes

MEASUREMENTS

3 teaspoons = 1 tablespoon

4 tablespoons = ¼ cup

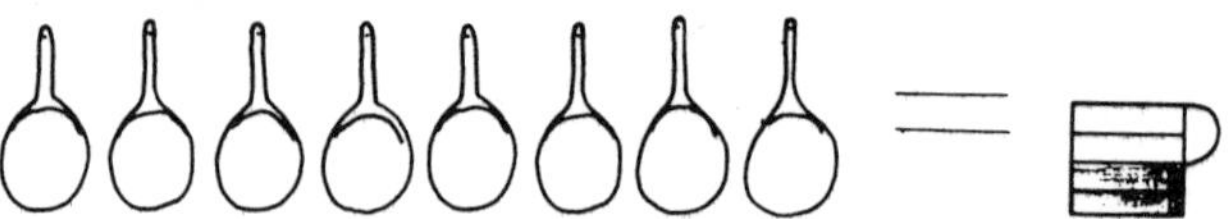

8 tablespoons = ½ cup

1 cube butter = ½ cup